The World Is Full of Pain

The World Is Full of Pain

Poems by

Anne-Marie Brumm

© 2022 Anne-Marie Brumm. All rights reserved.
This material may not be reproduced in any form, published,
reprinted, recorded, performed, broadcast,
rewritten or redistributed without
the explicit permission of Anne-Marie Brumm.
All such actions are strictly prohibited by law.

Cover design by Shay Culligan

ISBN: 978-1-63980-099-5

Kelsay Books
502 South 1040 East, A-119
American Fork, Utah 84003
Kelsaybooks.com

Acknowledgments

California Quarterly: "Apartment for Rent," "Monk by the Sea," "The Tree Massacre"
Canadian Women Studies: "Love in Tanka Time," "The Head of Holofernes"
CEA Forum: "At the Coffee Shop," "The Student as Poet"
Confrontation, "J.P. Morgan"
Carolyn Forché Prize for Humanitarian Poetry, Winner, 2019: "Letter From Oslo"
Generation: "Aloe"
Global City Review: "Ticking"
Iconoclast: "Doing Time for Love"
Jewish Currents: "2000 Dead, 5600 Wounded and…," "White Sheets"
Journal of Poetry Therapy: "The Art of Love"
Journal of the Altered States of Consciousness: "A Night at Eleusis"
New Outlook: "Stones Aflame"
Oasis: "The Commas of Jane Austen"
Orbis—Quarterly International Literary Journal: "Skogro at the Jazz Concert"
Paris/Atlantic: "Love, Death and Modigliani"
Paterson Literary Review: "City Scapes," "Media Widow," "Two Redheads at 38," "Virgins of Paradise"
Paterson Literary Review, Editor's Choice Award, Allen Ginsberg Contest, 2021: "At the Campus Bookstore"
Paterson Literary Review, Editor's Choice Award, Allen Ginsberg Contest, 2020: "Why My Mother Never Read Any of My Poems"
Pegasus: "Naomi and Najah at 17"
Poetica: "To a Young Man Dying of AIDS"

Poetry Quarterly: "A Poet's Lament"
Queens Quarterly: "Alexandria"
San Fernando Poetry Journal: "Homeless"
Voices Israel: "Coming Home," "The Commando's Tale"
Xavier Review: "Pavane for a Dead Princess"

Also by Anne-Marie Brumm

Dance of Life (poetry collection)
Come Drink Coffee With Me—Husband Hunting in Israel (novel)
Last Exit to Peace (poetry collection)
Honor Killing—a Mossad Thriller (novel)

Contents

The Night Scribbler	17
I Want to be a Lantern on Your Grave	18
Media Widow	19
The Beheading of Romina Ashrafi	20
The Heart Thief	21
Letter From Oslo	23
The Crush Box	24
Pantoum for a Paratrooper	27
Tadziu on the Podium	28
The Monk by the Sea (1809)	30
The Commando's Tale	31
Apartment for Rent	32
Aristeia	33
At the Campus Bookstore	34
Soccer Ball	35
To a Young Man Dying of AIDS	37
Coming Home	38
The Journey	39
Love in Tanka Time	40
The Ark of Alabama	41
A Poet's Lament	44
The Chess Game	45
Earth Dying	46
Adrift	47
The Writer's Lament	48
Love and Death on the Frisian Islands	49
Skogro at the Jazz Concert	50
Every Fifteen Minutes	51
Flight From Damascus	52
A Litany to Ban War	53
Take Just One	54
Three Haiku	56
Three Tanka	57

The Head of Holofernes	58
The Wedding	59
Has Anyone Seen Skippy Lou?	61
Winter Vistas	62
A Litany to the Lethe	63
The Peace Celebration	64
Coming Back	65
The Someday Times	66
Doing Time for Love	68
The Hero	69
The Forgotten Ones	70
The Tree Massacre	71
I'm Not in Love	73
Why My Mother Never Read Any of My Poems	75
Homeless in Winter	77
Two Redheads at 38	78
The Virgins of Paradise	79
Stones Aflame	80
2000 Dead, 5600 Wounded and…	82
City Scapes	83
The Commas of Jane Austen	84
Alexandria	85
Ticking	87
Pavane for a Dead Princess	88
Aloe	90
The Rite of Spring	92
White Sheets	96
At the Coffee Shop	98
The Student as Poet	99
Nightfall	101
Homeless	102
Scholar Emeritus	104

A Night at Eleusis	105
Love, Death and Modigliani	107
Naomi and Najah at 17	111
The Art of Love	112

*One word frees us of all the weight and pain of life.
The word is "love."*
—*Sophocles*

The Night Scribbler

"Don't let it go," my wise professor warned,
the thought that comes to you at night.
Idea, voice, plot—no matter how adorned.
Quickly heed its whisper, lest they all take flight!

Stumble to your desk, wake from sleep so deep.
Capture and chain it securely to your book.
Resist the urge to sink back into sleep.
In the morrow, all will be gone when you go to look.

One night, a story's clear form appeared to me.
I'll write it down tomorrow, I mumbled, closing my lashes,
snuggling back to sleep's sweet reverie.
The morning sun's violent light burned it all to ashes.

Now I eagerly hoist myself out of sleep-drenched bed.
My notebook filled with one-line wonders waiting to be bred.

I Want to be a Lantern on Your Grave

I want to be a lantern on your grave,
to keep a gentle watch when the darkness drops.
A light to fill the road your death has paved,
a throbbing rhythm when the pulse of time stops.

I will be the chief guardian of your absence.
I will write silent love letters and hope they will be read
and chase evil spirits, to vanish over the fence.
Invisible ropes pull you toward me but turn into a thread.

My thoughts of you tumble into many places.
I feel the deep silk of your voice but hear only sounds of strife.
I will soothe the pain of separation with the memory of your face.
The light will shine strong and save the brief illusion of life.

Grief is the price of love, Euripides once declared.
Love is a guest who visits only once. Be prepared.

Media Widow

I lived in the crevices of your life,
somewhere between Channel Two
programming, the film academy
and your latest documentary.
Like a gecko, I took on
the colors of your culture,
laid down my protest signs
when you said I was too visible.

I watched and waited
while you pitched at Cannes,
smiled at German producers
hoping to snare some funding
for your next feature.
Like a loyal caryatid,
I supported your ideas
and reined in your wildest plans
with tactful hints.

You carefully rationed your time
between me and the camera.
Yet I was content to sit
in the shadow of your screenings.
Last year, I applauded loudly
as you received a lifetime achievement award.
In the audience of the heart,
I deserved a front row seat.

The Beheading of Romina Ashrafi

Lamir, Iran, May 2020, Age 14

Can poetry describe such a hateful act?
A rose, asleep, is crushed by dad's cruel maim.
The moon hid the blade, the earth howled the fact.
A storm of teenage love, she needed to be tamed.

Her radiance was darkened, her fragrance turned to dust.
Did love transcend the strictures of belief?
Her love so forbidden, was the sentence just?
The tongs of tradition steal women like a thief.

Can love not flow freely like the stream?
Allow the graves reopened, their memory restored.
Tell the thousands martyred to live their dream
and a downpour of lilies fall from heaven's door.

If dad permits, girls 13, may wed.
But dad disliked boy's kin, so better to behead.

The Heart Thief

You entered the tollbooth
of my heart
without paying the fare.
You idled in its chambers
without permission or invitation.
You made my heart pace wildly
to meet the demands of your presence.
Not satisfied, you raced down
my arterial highways
heating my body to a boil.
You called it love.

My heart's traffic light told you, "stop"
but speeding way over limit,
you often crashed
leaving your marks of destruction
throughout my body—
the valves damaged, leaking,
leaving me breathless.
Sated, you returned on my venous parkways
with wastes
to my ever-forgiving heart.
Continuous round-trip journeys.
You called it love.

I tried to seal you
into one of my chambers,
but you seeped slowly into another.
When there was nothing left to take
from my bruised and battered heart
and better, more beautiful hearts, beckoned,

you took the nearest exit,
quietly and quickly,
without notice or apology.
I picked up the pieces.

Letter From Oslo

Dear Ali,
    I feel so all alone here. I have never known such cold. Don't mistake me. I am grateful that they let me stay and to the human rights worker in Tel Aviv who hid me when I ran there. He arranged for my asylum here.
    But I miss my family in Nablus, even though my father has threatened to kill me when he finds me. They have chosen a bride for me. I long for my beloved. I hope he is safe too and that we can be together again someday, somewhere. I dream of my tortured land, the olive trees, the orchards, my sheep. They are taking away more and more each day.
    What else can I do? Where else can I run?
                                  Be well,
                                        Samir

The Crush Box

Cambodia, Thailand, 2018

They call it the crush box
because that is what it does.
It crushes the body and mind.
Metaphors are not necessary
in this poem.
Comparisons to Dante's hell
are not needed.
This is hell!

It takes place in the entertainment camps.
The elephant is stuffed into an open box
and chained on all four legs.
Then, it is beaten from all sides
simultaneously for 24 hours.
The feet receive especially harsh whips.
The torture continues
until its brain is gone
and it cowers in helpless subjectivity.
Some require a repeat 24 hours or more.

Some elephants die in the process.
Some are killed for body parts.
Some are used to uncover land mines
from previous wars.

One goal is to destroy
the powerful instinct of mother
toward her baby.
She would do anything to protect it.
This bond must be annihilated,
completely obliterated at all cost.

After the beating, they are so bloody,
the baby does not recognize its mother.
When the elephant can walk by her baby
without recognition,
its mind has been blown.

The elephant is now ready
for logging, entertainment,
or carrying tourists for rides on its back.

When working, the elephants must often
trek long distances for many hours
without adequate food or rest.
When not working,
they are held in captivity,
their legs chained, like Prometheus,
by the gods of greed
to a rock of steel.

In their natural state,
elephants continuously roam in nature
and live in close family packs.
Now, their natural habitat destroyed,
they are unable to walk or interact with others.
They can only sway back and forth
as far as the chains will allow,
their large ears flapping.
It is the only way to cope
with the agony of confinement.
The swaying is an indication
that they are slowly going crazy.

But there is hope!
Sanctuaries to rehabilitate the abused animals
are emerging.
Mondulkiri is a good example and model
for others to follow.

Pantoum for a Paratrooper

It was you who volunteered
for the deadly suicide mission,
to save Jerusalem, the city that Herod built,
surrounded by an invading Arab army.

The deadly suicide mission,
ten brave men to jump from the sky
to fight the surrounding Arab army,
surprise their only weapon.

Ten brave men dropped from the sky,
a picture forever frozen in the history books.
Surprise their only weapon
to fight the fleeing Arab army.

You hoisted the flag on the Temple Mount,
a picture forever frozen in the history books,
you, 19, raising the flag on the Temple Mount
inside the city that Herod built.

Every year, on this day, a big parade
around the walls of the city that Herod built
to cheer the three brave men who survived
the deadly leap from the sky.

Happy crowds throng the streets
to honor the ten brave men who volunteered
their lives to give them back Jerusalem,
the city that Herod built.

Tadziu on the Podium

Every time I watch you lecture,
I think of Tadziu
on the Lido in Venice,
smiling seductively
from Visconti's screen.
His almost smile, backward glances,
so innocent they seem
yet promising vast vistas of paradise
if only I would follow.

We are all weary Aschenbachs
gazing at your exquisite angelic face,
straggly blond hair and aquiline nose,
searching for hope and beauty
in a decadent world,
seeking strength and inspiration
from your smoldering looks
for our unborn works of art.

O Tadziu on the podium,
standing confidently in contrapposto.
I am hanging on to your every word,
bedazzled by the seething power
of your convictions.
You play innocently
with powerful phrases,
ranting on about moral justice
and other complex concepts.

Then you end and walk away
like a Greek godling
into the water of life,
14 going on 40,

casting a playful backward glance.
You raise your right arm like Apollo
forever frozen in time.

I try to follow you
but lie dying on the beach.

The Monk by the Sea (1809)

a painting by
Caspar David Friedrich 1774–1840

A barely visible figure hovers
    at the edge of nature's immense expanse.
        He trembles at the thought.
            Soon he will be swallowed
                by the shadows of the approaching
            night.

He is helpless, insignificant, indistinct,
    as though he never really existed.
        Ghosts emerge from the darkness.
            Seagulls watch but are silent.
                The wind has ceased its caressing
    lullabies.

Only time is left to witness the scene
    the loyal, eternal, indestructible deity
        that leaves no footprints and no clues.
            Only the artist can create a canvas,
                with a figure that will stay forever.

The Commando's Tale

On October 10, 1973,
I killed a man.
I crept up behind him,
pressed my fingers on his jugular,
I hesitated for a moment.
He looked so much like me,
dark kinky hair, a moustache.
But I could not jeopardize the operation,
endanger my comrades.
And so, I pressed until his life was gone.

When all the guards had been killed,
the tanks moved in
and Jordan was neutralized.
After the war, they gave me a medal.
It lies somewhere in the drawer.

On the Sabbath, I take rides
with my wife and children.
When I look out at the barren
desert landscape,
I see his face everywhere.
Was he married? Had children?
What were his dreams?

Like Sisyphus,
I roll my rock of regret
up the mountain of mourning
but it keeps hurtling down
onto my wounded mind.
I try to ignore it
but it continues to crash.
Was it worth it?

Apartment for Rent

The apartment has been cleaned,
the owner declared proudly.
But stains of lost love linger everywhere.
The rooms are damp with cold secrets,
the walls sworn to silence
with the seal of confession.
They are bare but punctured with holes
like a ruined altar
where familiar pictures once hung
and were worshipped.

The shampooed carpets reek
of betrayal and bad sex,
the ceiling full of leaky hearts
begging to be patched up.
Each night, the garden roars
with revenge, pain etched deeply
into the wind that wails
like a chorus out of tune.
Once wired for life,
all utilities are dead now.

Plenty of closet space,
the owner boasts,
where angry spirits live on
as squatters, tenants that
can never be evicted.
They offer no hospitality and vow
to drive out all that is good.
The psychics warn that bad vibrations
may attach, hold on and destroy.
I thank the owner for showing.

Aristeia

*for all who died or were wounded
during the first and second intifada*

In the bright sunshine of manhood,
burning with virile youth,
you set forth to meet the enemy.
Your weapon a stone, your shield a kaffiyeh.

Tires smoking, roads blocked,
Suddenly soldiers, guns, jeeps.
Like an ancient discus thrower,
you hurl your stone
against fifty years
of suffering and servitude.
An answer of courage and pain.

But their guns aim carefully
and your moment of valor quickly ends.
You join the long list of martyrs.
Your bride waits, your children unborn.

Aristeia—from the Greek, a day of especial courage and valor of a warrior.

At the Campus Bookstore

It was there that we first met.
A warm and wonderful place.
How quickly I fell in love,
my whole life opening up.
Nothing would ever be the same.

Until we met, my life
was a boring and barren desert,
a lonely tenement in Brooklyn,
the school library bare.
I sneaked out to be with you.
My Puritan father disapproved.
Wasting time, he thundered
I could be working and making money.

Now my life is full and exciting.
Every day brings new surprises.
There is no going back.
Our bond is forever, I know
you will always be there,
a lighthouse for my ship.

Fyodor, Franz, Albert, Jean-Paul,
Lev, Alexander, Gustav, Federico
and so many others
waiting for me on the shelves
of my bookcases where they reign
like kings.

Soccer Ball

It had been so easy to snatch the gypsy boy
that night from their camp on Serbia's hill.
He's young and beautiful, for some a great toy,
the type tourists like, he'll be a great thrill.

We can sell him in Ljubljana for a good price.
So many tourists now looking for a nice piece of ass.
Will pay well too, whatever will suffice.
Rich Germans, so eager to buy as they slowly pass.

He looks sad, quiet, hope he's not sick.
When I open the car's door, he's hugging the ball
my son left behind. "Want to kick?"
I ask, waiting for my contact to call.

He's pretty good, fast, challenges me.
What a kid! He's quick like my son,
same age too, a great player to be.
There are big games to be won.

Hey, I almost forgot why we are here,
to pass him on the deadly journey.
I see him now as a real boy, someone dear,
not a something to be sold into slavery.

Suddenly I want to save him from his fate.
I quickly thrust him back into the car's seat,
so glad that my contact to pick up was late.
I drive away but too late, he arrives to meet.

He blocks my car. "What's going on," he cries.
"We had a deal. Hand him over or pay."
I'll never forget the pained look in boy's eyes
as he was pushed into the car and taken away.

"What have I done?" I wail. "Save my boy," I cry.
"I'll not do this again," I rail. "I'd rather die."

To a Young Man Dying of AIDS

for Isaac Rosenfeld
(1978–2003)

Searching for God, searching for Spring,
he lies hidden from the world,
hearing only muffled voices
from rooms he no longer enters.
Imprisoned by blurred memories
of a hot, humid summer when
craving the hemlock of love,
he stumbled into the steaming park.
Seraphic faces and sharp vodka
stilled the warning voice,
Thou shalt not lie with a man as…
In the morning, condoms found unused.

Now, mounds of quilts and blankets
cannot quiet the shivering.
Prayers smother in his sorrow.
Four walls, like a frame,
bind him to the rocky emotional bed
as securely as his namesake
was tied centuries ago.
But no angel comes to rescue,
no ram gets caught in the thicket.
He alone is the sacrifice.

Coming Home

We should have gotten him help
as soon as he got off the bus.

We should have seen the look in his eyes
as soon as he sat stone still at the table.

We should have understood his fear
as soon as he hid hours in his room.

We should have felt the grief in his being
as soon as he shut all of life's doors.

We should have placed him in a home
when we knew his mind was not the same.

We should have been with him
when he bought the gun.

We should have stopped him
before he pulled the trigger
to end the final battle.

But we wanted a hero,
a brave warrior in our midst,
laden with medals
returning in glory.

The Journey

Every summer, my friends and I
take a bicycle journey to a new place.
This summer will be no different
but we will go to Ostend in Belgium.
For, you see, this journey is illegal
in Germany.

My mother begs me not to go.
My girlfriend pleads, "Fritz,
you could still have another year."
But I don't want to be like my dad,
gasping for breath at the end.
So my decision is firm.
I will fight while I still can.
Amyotrophic lateral sclerosis is a cruel master.

I think I can make it but weaken
at the end and arrive by car.
We spend the last day at the beach.
The next day, we go to the house.
I am afraid, I admit.
The doctor is not there, he is ill.
A moment of hope floods my friends' eyes.
We must wait for another doctor.

Everything had already been explained.
I was asked again if I was sure.
I said, "yes" and hugged everyone goodbye.
I got into the prepared bed.
The doctor drew up the syringe.
"It will be quick now," he said
and injected the liquid into my vein.
I heard my mother gasp.

Love in Tanka Time

After the show, I
wanted to say I love you
but instead we talked
of your new CD, then
you drove away in your jeep.

Undressing myself
in words, for the world to read.
You never noticed
poised always on the narrow
catwalk of life, what I wrote.

Silence, tourniquet
for my overflowing pain.
Poetry, balsam
for my suppurating wounds.
Your love, a distant doctor.

Silence clusters warm
in the empty paragraphs
of life, hope shoulders
its way through shut doors filling
a wordy letter with love.

The Ark of Alabama

From far away
it looked like a large metal box
with specifications and dimensions
like the ark in Deuteronomy.
Where were the precious jewels?

The burly old man walked
bent forward like in Neanderthal times.
Soon he emerged from the back
with the jewels for the ark.
Yet he seemed oblivious to their value,
his stare robotic.

They tried to escape his cruel grip,
a cocker spaniel, two beagles,
the terrier struggled the most,
as if he knew.

He squeezed them all into the box
and with a paw-like motion
slammed the lid shut tight.

Then he hobbled over
to the dark green canisters
attached to the box and
lined up against the wall
like gaunt ballerinas
waiting for their cue.

He turned on the valve
and a hissing sound could be heard.

Soon screams filled the air.
The dogs crushed in the box
clawed against the walls
desperate to escape
gasping for the air
that was no longer there.

Some very long minutes passed
until only a few yelps remained.
Soon all was silent,
the temple service over,
the gods appeased.

Satisfied, Neanderthal then pressed a button
on the side of the box.
The lid sprung open
ejecting the dead bodies
into the back of a waiting truck.

He shuffled again to the back
emerging with the next batch,
the procedure repeated
until the truck was full
to ferry the furry bodies
to the landfill, no Charon
to safeguard their journey.
The earth would receive the sacrifice.

An efficient process, they swear,
clean, quick and quiet,
cost-effective too,
no medication or doctor needed.

Congratulations, Alabama!
Only you and Tennessee left now
loyal to the tradition.

Please accept this poem
as a Munch scream
to the deaf.

N.B. Information in the poem was obtained from the documentary film *One Nation Under Dog,* directed by Jenny Carchman and Ellen Goosenberg Kent in 2012.

A Poet's Lament

I look at my poems lovingly.
They have so much to reveal
but no one is listening.
The words are confessing their sins,
their heads bent in repentance
but no priest will give absolution.
The rhymes plead, "I want to comfort you"
but no one is buying.
The stanzas bleed too, their lines trapped
by the bottom line and inventory reports
but no one is helping.

No eternity is in sight,
not even a fiery hell.
What will happen to them when I die?
What fate will befall them?
What games will take their place?
My poems will exist like tree stumps
their forest glory gone
just languishing then for final removal.
The developer waits,
scales of greed clouding his eyes,
a business model in hand.

The Chess Game

Life is like a chess game,
full of moves, good and lame,
hurtling into one another blind,
no pause or plan in mind.

We try to choose what's next,
convinced we have the text.
Our vision small, the time so brief.
Our lives skid off a hidden cliff.

One can never know
the many roots a move may grow.
Hindsight holds the rocky road so fast.
Too late we see the paradise we passed.

If only to go back in time
and change the false and foolish mimes,
erase the hurtful words and deed.
Another chance to play the lead.

Earth Dying

It's happening quietly
barely noticed by those
who choose not to look.
The hymen of innocence
gone forever.
There are no poems here.
Decay cannot rhyme.
A permanent silence
will replace the hum of life.

Can the stem cells
of civilization
come to the rescue?
Or will our little earth
fade into the galaxy
like a wallflower
at nature's last dance?

Adrift

He nervously hurries
down a fog of avenues
forever leading nowhere.
It is no dream
when he slams into a painful reality
of colliding routes.

The rooms have no doors,
the showers no curtains,
the naked walls bear no mirrors
that could teach the truth
to the troubled teens
in this dark autistic ward.

Their minds are clogged
like a Celtic psalter
endlessly repeating
its cryptic message
in a language
no one can decipher.

A deviant world
hidden from view
like stalactites
in an ancient cave.
A permanent disconnect.
No light will enter here.
Outside lies a manicured landscape.
Rows of obedient flowers
bow their heads in unison
and frame the brief interlude.
Trees at attention
threaten the visitor.

The Writer's Lament

Laboring in the field of words,
the scribbler reaps a scant supply.
Surrounded by vultures
who seem eager to help
but only rake in large fees—
publicists, publishers, book doctors,
conferences and contests,
scammers of all stripes
promise the moon but sprout
long-winded weeds.

Yet he plunders on,
trudging through an avalanche
of rejections and empty husks.
Exhausted, he farms on hope and dreams,
poor nourishment for a fertile mind.
Defeated by his passion for the poem,
a prisoner to his addiction,
he cannot stop.
Most wither by the wayside
of this barren soil.
A few survive to warn and tell the story
but starry-eyed hopefuls and
besotted beginners will not listen.

Love and Death on the Frisian Islands

Albino sand and nimbus sky, an ashen frame
for a Frisian sea. Gray waves tower above
the stone dike's slanted back to tame
the restless waters, seeking crimson nights of love.

The sea, blushing with passion in the chill of night
waiting like a shy medieval maiden for love so near.
The dike is sworded in-between and love takes flight.
Some say, on nights like this, the dead appear.

The pallor of his face glows as the moon-drenched waves arise.
The aged rider whips his palomino along blankets of white,
the marsh sickness gaping from his sunken eyes.
Come to me, the sea whispers softly slumbering in the night.

The pale horse plunges over the dike's edge unseen,
finding Death's dark veil forged in-between.

Frisian islands—off the coast of northern Germany, Holland and Denmark
Marsh sickness—a colloquial term for cancer on the Frisian islands
The dike—a modern version of the medieval "chastity belt"

Skogro at the Jazz Concert

She enters in playful innocence,
caresses the microphone
with her silky voice.
She asks for response
but they sit stone still,
hypnotized by her Sirens' song,
too captured to applaud.

He is pagan
like Holofernes,
beguiled by her beauty
and smoldering Semitic eyes,
drugged by her deep tones.

He wants to lie forever
in her arms
but fears she will throw the ax
while he sleeps.
Or will she let the o'yev
Become the o'hev?
Will she rewrite history
for him?

In Scandinavian mythology, the skogros are beautiful and sexy nymphs with long and thick red hair. They lure men into the forest, seduce them, then kill them.
o'yev—Hebrew for enemy
o'hev—Hebrew for lover

Every Fifteen Minutes

My name is Setao.
Sorry, I can't talk long.
They may come back for me.
I live in fear.
I lost my whole family.
They shot the baby first,
so we would gather around
to save him,
then they killed my mate and siblings.
I was shot too, but survived.

Their heads are gone,
their splayed bodies stain the arid land.
It's our tusks they want.
They are valuable, it seems,
status symbols in Chinese homes,
or bring back young stud days.
So I live in fear, my tusks are long,
almost touch the ground.

We are gentle, intelligent beings,
close to our families.
Every fifteen minutes,
they kill one of us.
The wind, our only witness.
Many grow rich from the killings,
poachers, corrupt officials, buyers.
It's happening all over Africa.
Soon we will all be gone.
Who will save us before it is too late?
Who will mourn us?

N.B. Setao was killed in 2015.

Flight From Damascus

for refugees everywhere

Their voices shrunk to whispers,
families panic in their haste to flee,
fear their only compass.
The earth simmers under the soles
of their blistered feet.
Everywhere houses explode like nightmares.
Children coming, crying, crumbling.
Bullets, bottles, bombs fall heavily
as they burst through the air.
Smoke stretches its thin arms
blindly beseeching the dark silent heavens.

A slum of sounds spurts forth
from crowded tents.
Bodies ache, weary, lost,
their lives scourged of meaning.
Only bitter memories
soil their belongings.
Prayers shiver through the night.
Nervous laughs, sighs, tremble and die.
Stars smile, watching.

Now, as they wander amid
the strange, new streets of life,
will souls chiseled
in this furnace survive?
Time will fold their journey
into darkness.
Their voyage across sea and sand
will leave no footprints and no clues
for the centuries.

A Litany to Ban War

Minds tonged by hate, deliver us
Egos drunk with power, deliver us
Mirrors of hell, deliver us
People slotted in cells of fear, deliver us
Mired in mudholes of misery, deliver us
Ravished flowers of children, deliver us
Cultures scourged of meaning, deliver us
Raging hives of humanity, deliver us
False Messiahs everywhere, deliver us
Volcanos erupt with madness, deliver us
Poisoned soil screams with anger, deliver us
Despairing souls simmer in silence, deliver us
Dishonest men make deals in Hades, deliver us
Peace burns on the altar of lies, deliver us
The "Powers" prepare the holocaust of the cosmos, deliver us

There are no more words here.
Emptiness cannot rhyme.

Take Just One

Take just one,
the first one on the "euth" list,
the animal rescue volunteer begged.
But no one listened, no one cared.
People hurried by, encased
in their own lives and problems.
I saw a sad Siberian Husky
lying quietly in his cage.
He's sick and old, a worker
commented carelessly.
His dark brown eyes stared at me
as he begged for his life.

What would my mother say, the neighbors,
if I brought home another dog?
I took him outside for a walk.
He perked up and began to play.
His eyes held a glimmer of hope.
I thought how lucky I was
to be with him in the fresh air.
How lucky to be able to take him home!

If only many decades ago,
each person had taken just one
off the list and out of the cage,
the old and the sick
with their sad and sunken eyes begging.
But Roosevelt didn't listen, Churchill
didn't hear, so many were silent.
What will people say, what could happen
if I hid some Jews?

So no one came to open the cages.
There was no walk, no ray of hope.
No one came to take just one
out into the fresh air.

Three Haiku

lunging waves are tame
      in slate-colored photographs
           yearning to reach shore

a summer crowd chants,
      hot rock concert in the park,
           thick trees hide bored guards

bulging desk drawers,
      unpublished novels cry out,
           "I want to be read"

Three Tanka

Germany, 1941

Desperate to escape,
Jews give all for fake I.D.'s.
Relieved, they run fast.
Bullets to their heads follow.
Smugglers gloat and get rich quick.

Don't Bang on My Heart

Louisiana,
Twenty-five thousand dogs killed
each year in shelters.
First, they are sedated, then
a huge hammer hits their hearts.

Change

New computer comes,
trusty loyal typewriter
thrown into the trash.
I stand at the edge of life.
I fear, what will be my fate?

The Head of Holofernes

Prozac can consume
the flames of purgatory.
Only death doth drown
the fires of hell, the place
where crimson-haired Judith dwells.

The Wedding

The bride is Palestine,
the groom, the martyr
who has died for her.
Buried in his bridegroom's clothes,
he is forever married to the land.
A blood-soaked earth
trampled by tanks
and soldiers' boots.

Unborn children join him
in the grave.
They cry but no one
hears them.
He is the second in his family
to marry this way.
The parents, both proud and sad.
The reception, a time for
communal mourning.

Soon your face appears
as a mural on walls of buildings
and warehouses
throughout the area—
the colors, deep and defiant.
The tragedy wakes the sky,
sore with red welts
like a tortured prisoner's body.
Flowers adorn the tombstone.

There have been so many weddings
like this.
When will they end

and more real weddings begin?
Palestine—say it in a whisper,
the land that exists
only in memories and dreams.

Has Anyone Seen Skippy Lou?

Has anyone seen Skippy Lou?
We must find her.
She's a small blond terrier,
very shy and sweet,
wearing a pink collar.
Last seen at the medical offices building
in early February.

We must find her.
Her owner is very sick.
Full of cancer and chemo,
she needs her little dog,
her only comfort.
Please help us look for her.
Big reward.

If you see her, please call
646-416-8998 or write
marylouevans@gmail.com
102 Kerry Drive
Twin Oaks, Tennessee

Winter Vistas

a snow-drenched morning,
      stern-faced mother yanks stiff comb
            through my thick wet hair

cold winter night,
      I won the lottery but
            you return my gifts

thickening snow mounds,
      two lovers shovel and fight
            over summer plans

distant winter sun,
      I am waiting for your call,
            clouds hide the quiet

winter's ice-cold blade
      won't shave the thickened growth
            from your heart.
                  Will spring soften through?

A Litany to the Lethe

O River of Forgetfulness, could you please erase
the false pathways I have paced.
Another chance I'd like
to change the choices and make them right.

Caring parents would be a start.
Good schools, too, could play a part
to make life's rocky roads more smooth,
to dull the edge of saddened moods.

My hemlock now is Mahler's Fifth,
Debussy, Ravel, too, may be adrift,
to cushion cruel and painful worlds,
to stop the mind's obsessive swirls.

Mystery novels, foreign films dull life's daily pain.
My own words help to coat the heavy chain.
I discard lovers who control and abuse.
I search for a soul to serve as Muse.

The poor swim upstream all their lives,
young Goethe wrote in words so wise.
The rich glide easily down the river's course.
They do not need to take or force.

O River of Forgetfulness, if only you could knife
the painful choices of my life.
I thank you for your kind erasures.
There could not be more greater treasures.

The Peace Celebration

Everyone is invited.
West Bank teens burst balloons
instead of bombs.
Israeli soldiers fire bonbons
instead of bullets.
Gaza men shoot graffiti
instead of missiles.
Helicopters ignite fireworks
instead of flares.
The wounded recover and
get up to dance.
Suicide bombers return and
flirt with earthly virgins.
Falafel and schwaerma are shared by all.

Netanyahu dances "orientale"
with Nazrallah, while Abu Mazen
joins the hora with Miri Regev.
Darwish and Oz return and give
a joint poetry reading.
West-Eastern Divan Orchestra
plays an afternoon concert.
Settlers and local Arab youths
volunteer for the clean-up committee.
Trump joins Ahmadinejad
in closing prayers for peace.

Perhaps…someday??????

Coming Back

The Dawsons of Boca Raton
waited anxiously at the gate.
The plane from China had landed.
The gate opened
and he came bounding out to them
as though he had known them forever.
It was their beloved dog, Lancelot.

But wait, Lancelot died last year.
Then, who is this?
It looks like Lancelot, acts like him.
It is he.
The Dawsons are happy,
the DNA sample successful
and $150,000 well spent.

But I am still waiting.
When will the gate open
and my beloved Michael
come rushing out to me?
How much longer will it be?
And how much will I have to pay
for a film icon and national hero?

The Someday Times

I am a loyal subscriber
to the someday times.
They were the happiest ones.
One can live on hope.

I buy posters too large
for my miniature studio
for someday when I will have
a big house…
I save articles and brochures
about exciting places,
for someday when I will have
time and money to travel…
I buy a queen-size bed
for someday when I will find
and marry my soulmate…

I save all my old clothes
for someday they could be valuable,
be in style or even fit me again…
I keep a soft leather notebook in my drawer
filled with one-line ideas
for someday when I will make them all
into scholarly articles or literary novels…
I keep all my old lecture notes
for someday when I will find
another teaching job…

I keep all my old address books
for someday when I will rekindle
lost friendships…

I keep old copies of unpublished
manuscripts and poems
for someday when I will find
an agent or publisher…

Today is my birthday and I am sad
for someday is fading fast,
an impossible illusion beyond my grasp.
All that exists in my studio are useless dreams
the management calls
clutter.

Doing Time for Love

Locked in the prison of my body,
I received a life sentence
without parole, or so it seemed,
you being the righteous judge.

You fluttered through me
like a breezy, beach-filled summer
while I drowned
in the ocean-deep waters
of my wounds.

But now, a last-minute reprieve,
a possible escape beckons.
Release seems only moments away.
But I fear to leave my emotional cell,
the pain now familiar, a faithful friend.

The time has come to return
to life, my sin of loving you redeemed.
Freedom shines like a beatific vision
and I walk through the gate.
What rapture! What bliss!
You are gone!

The Hero

Once he was a hero,
admired by friends and family.
Only 14, he dared to throw stones
at armed Israeli jeeps and soldiers
with his slingshot. Rioted
in Jenin, protested at the border.

Such courage, but one time
a rubber bullet pierced his back
while running away
lodged in his spine
and rendered his legs useless.

Now he sits in the dark
in his heavy old wheelchair.
The electricity in his village cut.
No one visits anymore.
Medical and social services limited.
Weary and wounded,
tormented by regrets.

There are thousands like him,
victims of the intifadas.
Lost eyes, legs, spirits.
Wasted lives, empty futures.

The Forgotten Ones

Clad in Creuza's mantle,
he dares to lift the ear of corn.
unlocking the secrets of Eleusis.
There are so many of them,
the silent ones,
nailed to a lifetime of hiding.
The good ones—loyal and true.
But who will believe them
when they assert their innocence?
Struggling to maintain the light,
they survive amid the dark forces
swirling around them.
Will there be sufficient oil
to keep the flame bright?
Vestal virgins have gone for more
but will they be permitted to return?
Or will the mantle burst into flames
and devour all.

Firgin music has been banned.
Ganymede has been set free.
The beach house is now closed.
The Pastor has returned.
The smoke has scattered
and a bridge is opening.
Soon it will be safe
to come out
into the fresh air.

The Tree Massacre

The trees are watching anxiously
as the developer comes
clutching his clipboard.
He glares at the lush panorama
swaying in the gentle breeze,
a paradise of green
but he sees only shopping malls,
high-end real estate and parking lots.

The trees are afraid
but stand tall
against the tyranny
that will befall them.
They have lived here hundreds of years,
some, perhaps for thousands.
They are innocent
but condemned to death, without a trial,
an execution without a crime.

The fateful day arrives.
They begin at dawn, the trees still asleep.
A large crew with state of the art tools.
They attack like a blizzard,
tearing into the brave, but helpless bark.
Some trees, now barefoot, try to run away,
but fall quickly, without their shoes of soil.
Root tips electrify and scream in pain
but their cries are muffled
by the torn soil,
so no one hears.

Tree after tree topples.
Entire generations wiped out in minutes.
Large trees their children surrounding,
die together bravely.
They lie, silent and still,
where they fell,
like dead soldiers
after a lost battle.

Broken limbs
that will never heal
lie scattered everywhere,
their wounds oozing
streams of sap, like tears.
Splinters of bark, orphaned leaves
hug their new home on the ground.
The chopping continues for days, weeks.
Raw sounds cry out
like an atonal symphony.
Soon there are none left,
not even to grieve or weep.

Where there was once beauty,
there is now blight.
I weep for what once was
and what is no more.
I don't notice the roots
lowering into my unconscious.

I'm Not in Love

*A popular song in 1975
by 10cc, a British band*

Just because
I stayed so long in Tel Aviv,
don't think it was to be with you.
I'm not in love, no, no.
I love the sea.

Just because
I walked so often by your house,
don't believe I hoped to see you there.
I'm not in love, no, no.
I like its Arab architecture.

Just because
I saw your film eight times,
don't conclude, I think you're great.
I'm not in love, no, no.
My review needed details.

Just because
I came to the theater at midnight,
it wasn't to check your programming.
I'm not in love, no, no.
I searched for a midnight show.

Just because
I begged for your autograph,
don't assume I think you're brave.
I'm not in love, no, no.
It would increase in value.

Just because
I wear your paratrooper wings
close to my heart each day,
don't go longing for forever.
I'm not in love, no, no.
I don't care about tomorrow.

Why My Mother Never Read Any of My Poems

When my mother was 98
and I was changing her diaper,
I asked her casually
why she never read any of my poems
(or novels or essays)
hoping perhaps to get an honest answer.
She looked angry and pained.
"I thought maybe if I don't look at it,
maybe you stop all that writing stuff,
sending around,
wasting time, wasting money."

There had been so many over the forty years.
How strange, not even one. Why?

At first I thought, lack of education,
just seven years in a peasant school house
but similar parents were proud to show
the simplest poem or story.
Perhaps poetry was too difficult.
Surely she will read my novel
but I found her reading a biography
of Joan Rivers while my novel lay on the shelf.

Finally, I asked a shrink for answers.
We talked a long time and there were
many reasons that soon became clear.
She wanted to keep me small and insignificant,
hence did not praise my grades or works,
wanted to keep me close by,
so bad-mouthed my dates and forbade
many social activities.

She was afraid success in writing
might take me away, once she even
made a blind date with a local boy
who was frugal and lived at home.
"You marry Eddie, you won't send around
any more manuscripts, he wouldn't tolerate that."

She kept grilling every time I sent out a paper.
When I explained that writing essays was part
of my college teaching job, her ready answer was,
"Well, if you taught in high school,
you wouldn't have to do all that writing stuff,
and you would make more money
because they have a good union."

The shrink explained further.
She doesn't care about you, the way
her mother didn't care about her.
Imagine sending a small village girl out at 17
to a foreign country to make dollars.
Perhaps this tragic event also
made her unable to empathize with others.
Perhaps you were just a vehicle for her
to avoid deportation or for your father
to escape the draft. Why are you an only child?
But that is all in the past.
She has achieved her goal.
You are close by now
ready to change her diaper.

Homeless in Winter

the flood has dried, but
      a small dog, Snowball, is lost
           and a young boy weeps

bright Sunday morning,
      caged dogs in city shelter,
           night coming for them

big blizzard beginning,
      a stray cat shivers watching
           people warm inside

large snowflakes falling,
      feral cats wild for shelter
           fleeing from their fate

large ice block breaking,
      abandoned dog is stranded
           drowsing into death

I will make shelters,
      tarp and bubble wrap outside,
           warm blankets inside.

Two Redheads at 38

In the Tei Aviv suburb—

Tank top, tight jeans,
the flame-haired singer
strolls in the evening cool
with her latest adoring lover.
They will celebrate the success
of her new rock CD.
Tomorrow she will perform
for thousands in the "amphi"
but tonight they return
to her villa gleaming white
stone in the moonlight
and make forbidden love.

In the Druze village—

Her suit was too short,
her hair too bright,
the brother, 19, declared.
Returning from abroad,
she spoke publicly on TV
about the money she'd brought back
to build a home for the aged poor.
And so, he used his army rifle
to restore the family's honor.
"She did not behave like her sisters."
"Women belong in the home," he said.
The army was silent.

The Virgins of Paradise

*For Ashraf Mehdi, 19 years old
died, September 26, 1993 Gaza*

Are they very beautiful, Ashraf?
Which one will you wed?
Fulfill the promise to your mother
        and choose!
Did they whisper syllables of love
        as you drove the explosive-laden car?
Did they hum the Sirens' Song
        luring you to kill
        and be killed?
Did they inject the opiate of illusion
        into your willing veins?

"One of God's soldiers," you called yourself
        "doing a difficult work."
Are you not weary of fighting?
Are you not longing for peace?
Are you not content making garments
        for others?
Oh, faith junkie! Where was God
        when it happened too soon?
Why did you not lead an earthly virgin
        into the field of flowers
        and from afar
        watch your car ignite the sky?

Stones Aflame

Intifada 1987-1992

                Tires burning,
                stacked barrels,
                              black smoke
stretches its thin arms
            blindly beseeching
                              the vaulted
sky swollen with vicious welts
                like the prisoner's body
                      Troops
of stones, bullets, bottles
            fire
                              through the air
Children
          coming
                crying
                              crumbling
From an unseen rooftop
            a petrol
                              bomb blurs
into flames
            Houses explode
                              like nightmares
Bedouin barley fields
                              scream
            with sprayed poison
            Electric flames
                              scorch
the youth's nerves
when forced to take
                              his flag
            from the pole
Schools are shut
            minds closed

Will tongues of fire
        glow
                          untaught?
            A raging
                          hive of humanity
            in a rocky landscape
                          terraced
with bitter memories
The earth
        simmers
                          with suppressed emotions
            A slum
                          of stones
lies heavy
            with unsaid words
The land begins
            to crackle
                  with anger
            heating
                          to a boil
as bare soles
                          are forced
to extinguish the flames
A culture
            scourged
                  of meaning
                          does not disappear

2000 Dead, 5600 Wounded and…

He had been lucky, they all said,
to get away,
his tank sitting at the rim
of the valley
when the planes hit.
But like Lot's wife,
he had looked back
at the burning furnace
where his unit was trapped.
A gnarling, whirling gush
of hellfire
attacking the dark silent heaven.
A picture he would see forever.

There was a price to be paid
for looking back
a god once warned Orfeo.
And so it was!
Now his mind stands
like a pillar pitted
against the small scenes
of daily life
blotting out their meaning.
He stares at his blank textbook,
the term's reports not yet begun.
In class, a murmur of unconnected words
and Syrian planes.
He wanders about the streets
of life,
the apocalyptic painting
from the Beka'a his only compass.
The shrink said
it would take time.

City Scapes

A culture clothed in Prozac armor,
its eyes blind to beggars.
Suffering spreads like a virulent cancer.
Ghosts fill the streets.
Billboards laughing, drink Pepsi
and join the NOW generation.
Black smoke trails from tall chimneys
hug in the mottled sky.
Birds scatter into the smog.
Ghettoes choke, clogged with crime.
Tired evening, the city drowses,
its dimensions defined by scars
and broken dreams,
the smell of exhaust pipes sicken.
Hard-faced girls on stilts solicit.
Soon the angry horns of despair awaken.
Newspapers, like gods
shout what will be.

The Commas of Jane Austen

In the tilth of a meager harvest
        the scholar reaps a scant supply.
                It's one of those things, you know.

Up or out; he had to go
        but he cared for the fruit
                and sighed as day ripened night.

Chrome hours blend with the hues
        of a slightly bent Muse
                pondering the past perfect verbs of Proust.

Now quiet birds in distant fields
        peck on outstretched arms
                in a stick.

Dead eyes
        reading the autumn leaves
                of his yellowed books.

Alexandria

They call you "Alex" for short,
  Silver city of the night
    where life races
      without rhythm or rhyme.
        Winding streets and blind passageways
          hurry here and there
            like an unfinished poem.
              Soft murmurs vanish into mysterious alleys.
                Clots of people cluster everywhere.
                  Sudden courtyards hiding
                    beautiful madonnas and bronze colored babes.
            Scalloped coastal bays spin
          an endless sun intoxicated beach
        where crowds tide in and out
      with the sea.
    The Nuzha Gardens hang heavy
    with oversized blooms and pink birds
  in golden cages.
Modest sidewalk cafes
  boasting menus in French
    filled with idle men staring greedily
      as blond tourists mini by.
        Gaunt teenage girls saunter
          awkwardly in tight Italian spikes,
            hugging elegant little bags
              with fake Paris labels.
                They promenade new dresses,
                  bleak imitations of the latest chic
                and lower their dark eyes
                heavy with German multicolor mascara.
              Young men arm-in-arm walk three abreast.
            Discotheques scream the new western music

colliding with the arabic sound of centuries.
In Cafe Lucia, a writer once distilled
your exotic essence,
O ancient and modern metropolis!
Traffic ignores red and green
soaring down the wrong lane.
Donkeys and taxis compete for space.
Streetcars choked with humanity
enter the maddening daily race
then neigh to a sudden stop.
Bodies flit like flies
from the roofs and sides.
Ancient Roman theaters host
forgotten tragedies for tourists.
Catacombs exhale the air
of silent centuries.
Synagogues shrouded in stillness,
well-kept museum pieces now.
On Friday eve, a few aged souls
sit and remember.
Mosques mushroom everywhere
flowing over with male worshippers.
I live in the golden city
of the morning
but in the dark alleys
of my dreams
I long for you
and whisper
"Iskandaria"

Ticking

in an inner harness
of silence
a well marrowed secret
contentedly waits
propelled toward the palaver
of foreign guests.
The flicker throbs quickly about
but the mind tattooed
from remote designs
feels fleshless.

I pour libations
on the Ara Pacis,
a golden dolphin glides
toward an unsuspecting sub.
Closer…
The ambassador pledges a toast:
Chortling at the yellowed words,
a maw gapes
as a fiery burst flails the room,
a starched apparition spatters
into a dark cinerous hell.

Pavane for a Dead Princess

for the world-weary

From far away
    it looks like
        a winter agon,
an academic combat
    where both gods are sterile
        and never breed a spring.

In cold celestial colleges
    rituals play
        without religion.

Ichor flows
    as power is forced to be
        wisdom's fevered mentor.

Two now shiver in a barren core

An aging mill
    turns the
        department's tragic discotheque.
An insecure wheel
    furrows an untenured path
        toward an intolerable awareness.

Boy embraces girl—a moment passes
Non-being enshrouds Being—an eternity flashes

The earth reels
    as heavenly caryatids
        are lured to the frenzy.
Dancers bombard about
    propelled
        by the firgin music.

Life's record moans
        each night it yields
                to the needle worn
by torn myths of ivy
        spinning before waltzing
                glaciers of silence.

In the mirror
        I watch you incant
                ever stranger, stronger substitutes

while around the globe
        unseen galactic clusters
                gracefully glide
in a pavane
        for a dead
                princess

Aloe

Unseen in the grass, shunned and trodden
on by many, you root dormant in
the dusk of your skin. In a caul
of dirt, wilted on a listless
afternoon in sunny Washington
Square Park, you will
almost pass for a weed.
A sullen expression
pollens the splayed
mass of you. Bored
you pick up your
reed and begin
to grow as
you blaze
into a heavenly
cornucopia,
a slum of notes
spurts forth
whiffling
into a panic
of sounds
winging afar
as you kite
toward the sky.
Crowds gather
around the broken
bench, now a
sylvan shrine
where tongues of fire
burn untaught.
Poetry emanates
from the sunlight

of your mind
as night ripples
over the keys of an
angelic horn
Frenzied notes
epiphany
in the bloom
of the golden flower
that mouths your
saxophone
Harlem nightingale!
I flew after
the jetting tones
with my net
but captured
only a
dolmite of
silence.

The Rite of Spring

for David

I. On the Bench

It was no accident
or twist of fate
that hot July eighth.
I wanted to dance
the rite of spring with you.
Many seasons have gone by
and still I wait.
Come now, let us sway together
like waves in the moonlight.
You have inspired me to sing.
My small starved voice
cries to talk with you
but you are too busy to hear.
May these words of poetry
find a door
to enter you by!

II. The High Priest

David, your name
two syllables always on my lips.
The sun unveils
the mystical charm
of your face sculptured
by Praxiteles
and chiseled to perfection.
Your eyes bursts of burning brown
flash with fierce intensity,
the long dark lashes
sweep heavenward

twinkling like a Russian melody.
Your naked body, tall and strong
like the tower bearing your name.
But I am too shy to touch.

III. The Maiden

During the night I burn
like a poppy field
in bloom
ready to be scratched.
The silent stars watch
as I dream of you
entering my room
but it is only a mirage.
In the mornings
I lie awake
like a rosebud
wet with dew
waiting for you
to teach me
the mysteries of love.
But I languish alone
in my virgin limbo.

IV. The Thaw

Let us dance
to the raging rhythms
of Stravinsky.
The music's dissonant chaos
an echo of our inner confusion.

Let us create
an even greater storm
that will silence
the space of centuries.
The presence of strange feelings
pass between the lashes
of our eyes,
feelings that scorch me
like lightning.
Adonis, beloved of Zeus,
you have cast a spell on me.
Peripheral intellectual discussions
you think is my wish from you.
O, my Phoenix,
you are afraid of me,
little Diana, the virgin huntress,
the independent feline that walks alone.
I am afraid too, of the dark
so I hear only empty echoes
instead of songs of love.

V. The Sacrifice

You have awakened me from sleep.
Let the clouds come
and be our costumes
wrapping themselves
around our cave of love.
Let the passion of primitive Russia
trumpet through its pagan rite.
Come, I have chosen you
from thousands.

Hurry, the fire is ready.
Offer me to the gods
so that the land may bloom.

White Sheets

A white sheet
       flutters
              from the window.

What does it mean?

White wash of a '60s student
waging an innocent war
from his dormitory window?

Or is it a vision
of a sunny peasant village
hiding in the south Italian air?
You, she and a flapping sheet
tell the world
of a wedded night of bliss.

Or is it perhaps a symbol of peace
from a Palestinian village
in southern Lebanon
begging Israeli troops
for mercy?

Or is from the procession
after a wedding in Marrakech
the sheet fresh with blood
from the bridal chamber
held high on a pillow
for all the village
to see.

Or is it like a mirage
floating from the rooftop
of a Bedouin hut
in the Negev desert?
letting all travelers know
of a young virgin inside
age 12 - 13
for sale
for a camel
or (if she is *very* pretty)
perhaps for a cow.

At the Coffee Shop

Thoughts
      stuttering in your mind
hesitate to speak.
You sit down next to me
      wearing the cloak of a weary day
and an exhausted life.
I watch you drowning
      in the silence called manners.

The waitress misadds my check
      and you begin to vacuum your soul.
Passive,
I take in a waterfall of words
      about late classes and bad translations.
I listen
and hear you hovering
      near the cliff of forty
      fearing the edge.
Jagged ambitions cruelly chaff
      the reef of your success.

I see your face
      chiseled by refinement.
A snap sophistication
      marbles your restless waters.
I am chilled by you.

But then you feel
like a father
with a horde of PhD children
      to place in a withered world
      while you shadow about
      on rainy nights.

The Student as Poet

*for Alan, Fred, Tom,
Monica, Donna, Ronda…*

There's one in every class,
sometimes even two.
Like neon signs
in the Sahara,
they shine
amid the arid prose
of their classmates.
They linger after class
awkward in the shadows,
paralyzed by their anguish.
They come to the office
shuffling about
with nervous excuses.
You seem to meet them
everywhere,
the intensity of their feelings
charges the air
and frightens.

Their needs gape like wounds.
Sometimes they may even appear
slow or stupid.
Unaccustomed to their genius,
they are poetic adolescents
clumsily trying to write
with newly developed
emotional limbs.

Be patient!
They are flickering flames
seeking a waft of encouragement
to blazen into
raging fires.
They are mountaineers
trapped in the snowstorm
of their emotions
needing a kind but stern
mentor prodding them
to walk and fight
the desire to drowse
and die.

I know you are busy,
dear colleague
but do not lightly dismiss them.
They are worthy of your time.
Care about their little poem,
painting or song.
They may yet surprise
into well-adjusted productive
artists and you too
will have been a part
of creation.

Nightfall

The shadow of night steepens
        and seizes the retreating light.
                The sun has already escaped and
                      seagulls shout their last commands.
                              Ghosts emerge from the sharp-
                         tongued waves,
                                      somber soldiers of the sea.

The quiet sand standing guard
        slumbers now
                breathing the sultry warm wind
                        that marches through the sky.

Ceaseless lullabies leash their hushed
        harmonies onto the shore's soft keyboard.
                Time folds into the darkness
                        leaving no footprints and no clues.
                        We follow
                                    surrendering to the mystery.

Homeless

                Thirsting
                      in the cold moonlight,
oases
                of haunted eyes
                      stare into the tight
              darkness.
Profiles hiding their pain,
                hands with no concentration,
                      thoughts with no direction,
they huddle
                      stone still
                      slotted
                      in the corners
of Gan Me'ir
                    trapped
              in the vomiting wind
and rain
              raging
                    around them.
Life dozes
              under coarse blankets
                and shawls
                    of sand.
Their cries
            have not wounded
                    the darkness
            of silent complacency.
The stars overhead
            whisper
                    in syllables
           of fear.
Who are these new scabs
                    on the earth?
            cafes are thick

                        with talk
            and cinemas hum
                        with frivolous films.
What poet will write
            the saga
                        of this spectacle?
What artist will paint
            the pain
                        of this purgatory?

Scholar Emeritus

The castrati sing their scholarly tunes
before the convention's bleary audience.
They'll listen this time!
Tired residue of an overripe era.

Lofty sublime tones flower no more
from the sculptured stage
of scholars crouching with age.
Move on, mental vagabond,
through sterile negevs
covered with sand instead of shoots.

Limning another's fertile land,
your own plot once cried out "Sprout!"
But fixated in the glory of bygone days
you hoed aside the earthy voice.
Now with moles' eyes and nimble rachitic fingers,
you anoint each tome with reverent praise.
But the prayer is shriveled and the choir still.

A Night at Eleusis

The offertory of
centuries
                    past
lies in the dark tarn
              of Ibis,
a time for
     transubstantiation.
The Parsee lights
     the flames,
                his chimere
     billowing, a
Rossum acolyte assists
     in the winnow.
A reading from the book of
                       Kierkegaard
     asking
who could tolerate?
Mystae smiling
     with Eleusinian candles
     melt the pond's ice
A vapor of
     tarred
incense, and the chalice
     of your blood
                 warmed
for infusion.
Waiting cells stretch
     and relax in the
interstitial bath.

     Epopteia
He lifts them high
over a cockless coffin.

I watch
as you begin to stir
and slowly stand
                    in contrapposto
cordoned with life
    in a foreign century,
        you mumble in outdated babels.
Elina Makropulos screams "no!"
"It's a great mistake to live so long!"

Kiborions of love
obliterated
Mutates feared
but the process continues
while
        an aged Farmer
        in the swaying fields
        of Kansas
lifts an ear of corn
        to the sun
        and sees that
        it is good

---

[1] Epopteia—the highest part of the Eleusinian mysteries whereby it is thought that a reaped ear of corn was held up in silence for all initiates. The new crop was the symbol of the eternity of life.

Love, Death and Modigliani

In memory, Alexander

Time is long
for the dead,
even longer
for the living.

The dark streets still pace
by me as I walk,
seeing a blur of shadows.
Everywhere happy couples
with bouncing strollers.
Avoiding the trap of mirrors,
I no longer know
what I look like.

I would like to be whipped
and receive wounds
I could identify,
something to point to
instead of the terrifying
emptiness.

I feel like a stone
heavy on your grave
trod deep by memories
until I can almost
reach you.

Suddenly a Modigliani face
lurches out at me from the void.
It shudders and jerks away
realizing the snare
of the store's mirror.

Why must love end this way?
in a dark hospital ward.
Perhaps you cared too much—
too dedicated to the profession
of curing others.
Why, a thousand times, I ask
until the words
starve into an echo.

What is it like to he dead
anyway?
I am chilled by my ignorance.
What a short step
between life and death.
Suddenly you are permanently
cured of living.

Perhaps you are suffering
more than I.
Perhaps you are watching me
as I write this poem.
What do you think of it—
any answer will do.
But all I hear is an
anxious silence
which grows like a cancer.

I find myself rocking
like an abandoned tree
in the desert wind
weeping for you
and all for whom

death has boiled
in the blood
leaving not even enough vapor
for a ghost.

Everyone has to die, sooner
or later, the comforters say.
Yes, but not at thirty-two
not before one has loved
to madness.
Yet perhaps there is no reason.
Perhaps the gods are dead too
or just tired of pulling strings.
A huge practical joke.
Someday science will discover
that Hodgkin's Disease is caused
by green-eyed viruses
found in sugar cones.

And we will laugh
like stones.

```
                    Twilight
                  tolled hard as I
                pressed down the dank
              streets, factory and alley
             zigzagged by in long silence,
            a hippie, her little girl drag-
           ging approached to beg. Clusters
          of youths idling here and there. I
         see it from afar, the drunks splayed
        on the benches, garbage cans dancing
       in front of the once proud Episcopal
       church. I tiptoe    by as they sputter
       anchored in their   stupor, slip inside
       the tall black ga   tes open only to know-
       ing eyes.                Quietly I wade
       through the stalks  of nature's muffling
       debris past J.P.'s  grave and last weeks'
       flowers. The stone  breath of a shrouded
       world chills until  up the stairs into the
       turret, the "group" circled for the poetry
       workshop. Ted Ber   rigan was shuffling his
       notes, a crowd tense  to hear their own torn
       later. "Did you hear  Ginsberg was robbed a-
       gain last night?"   There was a housewife still
       trying inbetween the No-Doz, a staunch business
       man writing like J.P. shocked at the rest of us
       On Sunday afternoons, the tourists taxi by St.
       Mark's to see J.P., flit away when they see the
       bums                                           and
       the          J.P. MORGAN                     poets
       Some          1837-1913                       peek
       into                                            the
       jazz service in the nave, shake their heads at
       what it's all coming to and whisper how a guide-
       book ought to warn a body about places like this
```

Naomi and Najah at 17

Unmarried and pregnant,
only a few miles apart,
yet the distance of centuries
divides the two cultures.

In Tel Aviv, Naomi plans a big wedding,
a honeymoon abroad,
a new apartment awaits her return,
her child receives the rabbi's blessing.
She hopes for a boy
to serve in the army's elite.
Special bridal shops cater
to her growing womb.

In Iksal, unspeakable shame,
the family's honor disgraced.
Islamic law dictates the tragic end.
Najah is torched and burned,
father, brother, cousins do their duty.
The villagers watch the fire.
All traces of her removed
and forgotten.

The Art of Love

Love is
like a Roman painting—
dead-end alleys,
gardens of illusion and
blind rooms with windows
promising colorful vistas
leading nowhere.

Love is
like a medieval painting—
without perspective,
the figures askew
on a psalter thick with
strangled feelings.

Love is
like a modern painting—
without meaning,
incongruous bodies wake
to find themselves pasted
together, their bed
out of proportion.

Love is
like no painting at all
an empty canvas, the lovers gone
or perhaps they do not exist
waiting for the artist
to transform his agony
into the balsam
of art.

About the Author

Anne-Marie Brumm has written two other books of poetry and three novels as well as numerous essays about literature and film. She graduated from Columbia University and received a PhD in comparative literature from the University of Michigan. Her experience teaching literature and creative writing was at Kean University in New Jersey, Ben Gurion University in Israel and Albert Ludwigs University in Germany. In 2019, she won the Carolyn Forche Award for humanitarian poetry and in 2020 and again in 2021, she won an Editor's choice award in the Allen Ginsberg contest and also in 2021, her novel, *Devil in the Ivory Tower,* was a semi-finalist in the Elixir Press prose contest. She lives in New York City.

www.ingramcontent.com/pod-product-compliance
Lightning Source LLC
Chambersburg PA
CBHW070508090426
42735CB00012B/2700